THE BEDTIME SHEMA

Transforming sleep into a daily spiritual practice

PHILIPPE BENBASSAT

RABBI M.Z. RAPOPORT
17 Russell Gardens
London
NW11 9NJ

Tel: 020 8458 8471
Mob: 0797 151 8688

9th Tevet 5780

It is with great pleasure that I pen these words of appreciation and praise of my dear Brother-in-Law, Michael (Philippe) Benbassat Sheyichye, upon the publication of his manuscript "The Bedtime Shema: Transforming sleep into a daily spiritual practice".

Having read through parts of the manuscript, it is evident that he has invested much time and effort into researching our holy sources in its preparation.

The booklet masterfully encompasses the themes and ideas behind the Bedtime Shema, in a concise, well-structured and clear manner, giving us a deeper understanding of the Keriat Shema.

The booklet will no doubt make the Bedtime Shema a more meaningful experience for those who read through this Kuntras.

May Hakadosh-Baruch-Hu grant the author continued Menuchat Hanefesh to further spread the word of Hashem.

With admiration and Torah Blessings

Meir Zev

Rav, Imrei Shefer Congregation

This book is dedicated to the loving memory of

Rabbi Alan Cohen -

Avrohom Moshe ben Eliezer HaKohen z"l

An educator par excellence, a man who inspired many and lived with a love of true *Torah im derech eretz.*

May his legacy live on through his children, grand-children and great grand-children.

ACKNOWLEDGMENTS

The book is based mainly on a series of lectures given by Rabbi Yerachmiel Goldman (Baltimore Community Kollel) in 2016, which can be found on torahanytime.com. I am very grateful to Rabbi Goldman for allowing me to use his resources.

Other sources have been used in order to include information and explanations of the various traditions, thereby making it as inclusive as possible.

I am also very grateful to Rabbi Chaim L. Dagul (Kollel Zichron Shaul, Gateshead) for going through all the sources, his additional contributions and his editing skills.

Thank you to family and friends for reviewing the text and for their contributions and constructive feedback.

Last but not least, thank you to my wife for her continued support and encouragement.

January 2020 / Tevet 5780

TABLE OF CONTENTS

INTRODUCTION

CHAPTER 1 – RIBBONO SHEL OLAM - FORGIVE AND CONFESS

CHAPTER 2 – HAMAPIL

CHAPTER 3 - SHEMA YISRAEL

CHAPTER 4 – VIYHI NOAM

CHAPTER 5 – YOSHEV BESETER ELYON (PSALM 91)

CHAPTER 6 – MA RABU TZARAI (PSALM 3)

CHAPTER 7 – HASHKIVENU

CHAPTER 8 – HAMALACH HAGOEL

CHAPTER 9 – IM SHAMOA TISHMA

CHAPTER 10 – VAYOMER HASHEM EL HASATAN – DENOUNCING THE SATAN

CHAPTER 11 – HINEI MITATO SHELISHLOMO – SIXTY WARRIORS

CHAPTER 12 – BIRKAT KOHANIM

CHAPTER 13 – REFLECTIONS ON THE NUMBER SIXTY

CHAPTER 14 – HINEI LO YANUM - OUR GUARDIAN DOES NOT SLUMBER OR SLEEP

CHAPTER 15 – LIYSHUATECHA KIVITI HASHEM

CHAPTER 16 – BESHEM HASHEM ELOKEI YISRAEL – THE FOUR PROTECTING ANGELS

CHAPTER 17 – THE JEWISH HOME (PSALM 128)

CHAPTER 18 – RIGZU V'AL TECHETA'U - TREMBLE AND DO NOT SIN

CHAPTER 19 – ADON OLAM

CHAPTER 20 – VIDDUY

CHAPTER 21 – DAVID AND BATSHEVA (PSALM 51)

CHAPTER 22 – ANA BECHO'ACH

CHAPTER 23 – FINAL VERSES

CHAPTER 24 – PSALMS 1-4

CHAPTER 25 – HALACHIC CONSIDERATIONS

CHAPTER 26 – CONCLUSION

BIBLIOGRAPHY

INTRODUCTION

Everyone needs sleep. Our energy levels are limited, so even the strongest person cannot continue being active for 24 hours per day. Nobody is invincible, and sleep is necessary in order to be revitalised and refreshed.

Indeed, in the book of Job (3:13), it says: *yashanti az yanuach li* - I slept, then I was comfortable. The numerical value of the word *az* (aleph, zayin) is 8. This indicates that an average person needs eight hours of sleep at night.

Several studies and experiments have clearly shown that sleep deprivation causes discomfort, disorientation and various other health hazards.

With the exception of people who work on night shifts, people tend to sleep at night, which is a time of danger and vulnerability. Those dangers are both physical and spiritual.

Chazal (Sages of blessed memory) therefore instituted the bedtime prayers. As a minimum, one needs to say *Hamapil* and Shema. Over time, other verses were added. The Bedtime Shema is not a prayer that is said with a *minyan* but individually, alone in the privacy of one's bedroom. Therefore, different customs and versions have developed, even within the same *nusach*. For that reason, variations between Ashkenazi, Sephardi and other traditions are not noted here.

An additional purpose is so that a person goes to sleep with words of Torah on his mind. This will have a positive influence on his sleep and dreams. The Bedtime Shema is a preparation for the next day, meaning that the way we go to sleep affects the way we wake up.

Rabbi Abraham Twerski writes (Life's Blessings, p. 256) that the attitude with which one goes to sleep at night may well determine the attitude with which one awakens in the morning. If a person can develop the attitude that he or she wants to sleep in order to obtain the necessary rest for observing Torah and mitzvot, every moment of sleep can then be seen as a preparation for this. On the other hand, if someone looks forward to sleep as an escape from the stress and worries of the day, the very stress that he is trying to escape from is likely to confront him upon awakening.

The objective of this book is to offer some insights into the various parts of this prayer.

Most *siddurim* call the Bedtime Shema *'Keriat Shema Al HaMitah'*. However, some refer to it as *'Keriat Shema Sh'Al HaMitah'*. Both expressions have the same basic meaning.

CHAPTER 1: RIBBONO SHEL OLAM - FORGIVE AND CONFESS

The Bedtime Shema is the last activity of the day before going to sleep. One has to realise that there will never be another day like this day.

Therefore, most *siddurim* begin the Bedtime Shema with *Ribbono Shel Olam*. This is a moment of *cheshbon hanefesh* (introspection), when one can review the day and ask oneself what went right and what went wrong. Some people might even write down what sins they have committed in order to improve and refine their character. The hope is that tomorrow will be a better day. Everyone wants his or her life to become better.

One could expand this introspection by listing all the good things that happened, all the challenges and difficulties and finally by recording examples of Hashem's kindness that have happened that day. The point is to get a clear perspective of oneself and that day, where one is coming from and where one is going.

There are different versions of this prayer in various *siddurim*, even within the same *nusach*; words have been changed, added or removed.

Some *siddurim* do not contain the *Ribbono Shel Olam* altogether.

The version that appears in most *siddurim* comes from the *siddur* of the *Shelah Hakadosh*, where it states that this prayer has been transmitted over the generations since the early Kabbalists.

There are two parts to this paragraph.

In the first part, a person declares that he forgives anyone who angered him, upset him or sinned against him. The *Mishnah Berurah* (239: 9) writes, based on the Talmud (Megillah 28a), that in merit of forgiving everyone before retiring to bed at night, one will be blessed with a long life.

The second part is a general confession of sin, which is short and powerful. We ask Hashem for our sins to be erased, but not through suffering and pain. Some people recite the full *Vidduy* (confession) before going to sleep.

The following section explains the various phrases used in this prayer.

Ribbono Shel Olam – Master of the Universe.

We address Hashem here as the Master of the Universe, with His greatness and vastness. We are so small and vulnerable, making this declaration from our beds! At the same time, it also describes the closeness we can achieve with Hashem, even from our bedroom.

Aiming for closeness with Hashem is the essence of Judaism.

Mochel – Forgive.

We forgive everyone who angered, annoyed, upset, antagonised or even sinned against us. We do not want to bear a grudge or be angry with anyone, especially those closest to us, such as family, friends and colleagues. We do not want anyone to be punished because of us. We want to be forgiving people, thereby releasing ourselves from scrutiny as the Talmud tells us (Rosh Hashanah 17a, Megillah 28a), if someone overlooks misdeeds that others do towards him, Hashem forgives all his sins.

However, just because we forgive them, this does not necessarily mean that Hashem will forgive them. They need to repent in order to achieve Hashem's forgiveness.

Gilgul – Reincarnation.

Some *siddurim* omit this reference. This is understandable, as there does not seem to be much reason why a person should need to forgive people for sins they did against him in a previous incarnation every night. It would be enough to do so once in one's lifetime.

Although the concept of reincarnation is beyond the scope of this book, it is worth mentioning that another prayer where reincarnation is mentioned (in some *nuscha'ot*) is during Yom Kippur. In some traditions, the *al chet* confessions contain the phrase 'For the sin that we committed before you in this incarnation and in other incarnations'. A few lines later, it goes into more detail, saying 'For sins for which we are liable to undergo reincarnation as an inanimate object (e.g. a stone) or one that grows (e.g. a plant) or as a non-speaking life form (i.e. an animal) or as a speaking life form (i.e. a human).

Lechol Bar Yisrael- Every Jew.

This seems to imply that we are only forgiving fellow Jews, although the next sentence says that "no man (*shum adam*) should be punished because of me".

Some *siddurim* use the words *Ben Adam* instead of *Bar Yisrael*, which clearly alludes to an all-inclusive forgiveness. It could be argued that if someone wishes to ask Hashem for unconditional forgiveness, he should unconditionally forgive everyone, Jewish or otherwise.

The source of forgiving people before going to bed is the statement that Mar Zutra said when entering his bed (Megillah 28a): "I forgive everyone who upset me". This text does not specify Jewish people.

CHAPTER 2: HAMAPIL

The source for this blessing is the Gemara (Berachot 60b), which states that when a person is about to go to sleep, he should recite the first paragraph of the *Shema* followed by *Hamapil*.

There are variations in the *Hamapil* text between *siddurim*, with some versions closer to the text of the Gemara than others. Since the Bedtime Shema is an individual prayer, it is likely that variations developed over time.

Hamapil is a blessing on going to sleep. When we sleep, we cannot see or (knowingly) hear anything, so we do not know what is happening around us. We are weak and totally vulnerable. At the same time, sleep is an investment. After a night's sleep, we should be revitalised for the day to come. We are re-energised so that we can toil in Torah, pray, go to work, raise our children, etc. Going to sleep is therefore a gift from Hashem and is certainly worthy of a *beracha*.

Reciting *Hamapil* elevates the otherwise mundane act of going to sleep into a more spiritual experience because we are using sleep to connect to Hashem.

This blessing is very personal and acts as a link between our ancestors and ourselves.

In *Hamapil*, we say *Elokai velokei avotai*, my G-d and the G-d of my forefathers. We are thereby connecting to our parents, grandparents and the *neshamot* (souls) of previous generations.

We make the same connection in the first blessing of the *Amidah*.

The wording is clearly designed for the individual. It speaks about *my* eyes and *my* eyelids, *my* forefathers, lay *me* down to sleep, raise *me* in peace, *my* thoughts, *my* offspring, etc. Some versions though are in the plural, i.e. *our* eyes, *our* eyelids, *our* forefathers, etc.

The root of the word *Hamapil* is '*nafal*' - falling. Seemingly, this has a negative connotation. However, we are falling asleep because Hashem enables us to do so, he controls the state of our sleep. Chazal tells us (Berachot 57b) that sleep is one sixtieth of death. Hashem, so to speak, transports our souls to *shamayim* (heaven) while we are asleep, and causes us to wake up refreshed.

Chevlei shena - bonds of sleep. This means that our eyes are tightly closed when we are asleep and are even "bound" by the mucus that often forms in our eyes when we sleep. This expression is in the plural, thereby referring to the various stages of sleep (light sleep, REM, etc.)

Veta'amideini - raise me up. We are confident that we are going to wake up and that everything will be functioning again.

Ve'al yevahaluni ra'ayonai vechalomot ra'im vehirhurim ra'im - May my ideas, bad dreams and bad thoughts not confound me. This theme is also mentioned in *Ribbono shel olam* recited earlier. We do not want to have improper thoughts, even fleeting ones (*hirhurim*). The night is often a time when people are more vulnerable to being confused by deep thoughts and ideas (*ra'ayonai*), whether religious or philosophical. We therefore pray to Hashem that we should not to be confounded by such concepts. We can counteract this problem by occupying ourselves with positive thoughts before going to sleep.

We pray that we will be protected from bad dreams (*chalomot ra'im*). During *birkat Kohanim* on Yom Tov, many people pray that their dreams should have a positive outcome.

Mitati - literally, "my bed". This is a reference to our offspring. This is an opportunity to pray for children and to be mindful of their physical and spiritual wellbeing.

Mitati shelema - perfect offspring. This can also be a reference to Yaakov Avinu, who only had pure offspring, as opposed Avraham and Yitzchak, who also had less pure offspring (Avraham had Yishma'el and the sons of Keturah, and Yitzchak had Esav).

Veha'er einai - illuminate my eyes. When a person awakes in the morning refreshed, his eyes are bright. This is in contrast to when a person is tired, at which time his eyes are darker because the pupils are dilated.
Even at night, amid the darkness, Hashem provides illumination.

The *Mishnah Berurah* (239:2) brings three opinions when to say *Hamapil*: before *Shema*, after *Shema* or at the very end of all the prayers when one is about to fall asleep.

Some say that since *Hamapil* is connected to sleep, it is best to say it at the very end, so that there will be no interruption between saying *Hamapil* and falling asleep.

Others argue that since *Hamapil* is part of the core of the Bedtime Shema, it is best to say it at the beginning (before or after *Shema*). They also maintain that the verses said after *Shema* do not constitute an interruption.

The *Mishnah Berurah* does not issue a ruling about this. People should either follow their fixed custom or act according to their own capabilities. For example, if a person tends to fall asleep while reciting the additional prayers, he should say *Hamapil* beforehand.

Some people recite the blessing without *Shem umalchut* (Hashem, King of the universe). A person is not supposed to talk after finishing the Bedtime Shema. This is particularly the case after reciting the *Hamapil* blessing, which is meant to be said immediately before going to sleep. However, sometimes people need to talk after the Bedtime Shema for reasons of *shalom bayit,* because children wake up or for other reasons. If this is the case, it may be preferable to omit *Shem umalchut* from the *Hamapil* blessing.

The *Poskim* discuss various reasons as to whether or not *Shem umalchut* should be said. They also discuss whether *Hamapil* is a blessing recited on the act of going to sleep or on sleep itself.

The *Kitzur Shulchan Aruch* (71:4) writes that *Keriat Shema* and the other psalms and verses should be said before getting into bed and the blessing of *Hamapil* should be said while in bed. Before going to bed, one should walk over to a mezuzah, place one's fingers on it and say *Hashem Shomri*...("Hashem is my guardian") . This is identical to the verse in Tehillim 121:5, except that the verse in Tehillim is said in the plural, and *Hashem Shomri* is said in the singular. Afterwards, one should say *Bechol Derachecha*... ("In all your ways, know Hashem" - Mishlei 3:6) seven times. This is not generally mentioned in *siddurim* and does therefore not appear to be a widespread practice.

If a person cannot fall asleep after finishing the Bedtime Shema, he could repeat the *Shema* while meditating on the words, their meaning and spelling or think about the individual letters forming the words.

It is interesting to note that in the morning , we say a blessing thanking Hashem for "removing sleep from my eyes and slumber from my eyelids" (based on Gemara Berachot 60b). In many respects, this blessing mirrors *Hamapil*.

CHAPTER 3: SHEMA YISRAEL

It is beyond the scope of this book to describe the *Shema* in full. We will therefore limit ourselves to the aspects pertaining to the Bedtime Shema.

Not all *siddurim* include the three paragraphs of *Shema*. Many *siddurim* only contain the first paragraph. The original custom was to recite only the first paragraph, as stated by Rashi and Tosafot at the beginning of Berachot (2a).

The *Shulchan Aruch* (235:1) writes that if a person *davened* (prayed) Maariv before halachic nightfall, he has not fulfilled the biblical obligation of reciting Shema. Therefore, he has to repeat the full Shema after nightfall. The time of the Bedtime Shema is an opportune moment to do so if he has not done so earlier. If someone wants to fulfil the biblical obligation of saying *Shema* at this time, he must have in mind that he intends to fulfil the mitzvah.

If a person davened Maariv after nightfall, it is sufficient to say the first paragraph of *Shema*. It is however preferable to read all three paragraphs in order to protect the 248 limbs of the human body (*Mishnah Berurah* 239:1).

When saying the full *Shema*, one should first say *Kel Melech Ne'eman* in order to say 248 words, corresponding to the 248 limbs. *Kel Melech Ne'eman* should not be said when reading only the first paragraph.

Some people do not say *Kel Melech Ne'eman* but instead repeat the last three words in order to reach 248 words.

The Mishnah in Oholot (1:8) lists the 248 limbs of the body that can convey ritual impurity. They are found in the feet, legs, pelvis, ribs, hands, arms, shoulder, spine, neck, head and various openings and orifices. These limbs (from a human corpse) transmit ritual impurity when a person or object touches them, carries them or is under the same roof or canopy as them.

The *Zohar*, in *Parashat Vayishlach*, says that a person has 248 limbs in his body, corresponding to the 248 positive commandments in the Torah. Rabbi Chaim Vital expands on this by describing the physical and spiritual limbs and how the performance of mitzvot creates a connection between them.

The Gemara in Nedarim (32b) teaches us that the numerical value of Avraham is 248, symbolising the fact that Hashem gave Avraham mastery over all his limbs.

Ideally, every word of the *Shema* should be said with *kavanah*, with concentration and focus on all the limbs.

The Rambam writes (*Sefer Hamitzvot, Mitzvat Asei* 3) that it is a mitzvah to love Hashem. When contemplating every part of creation, whether it is majestic mountains, the vastness of the seas and oceans, a night sky full of stars, the role every creature has in this world, the intricate constitution of living beings, etc., a person cannot help but love Hashem, wish to praise him and want to connect to Him even more.

Although we can never really know Hashem, we can certainly contemplate His greatness and infinite wisdom.

Those thoughts may not necessarily induce sleep, but they are a very positive and exalted way to connect to Hashem.

Part of the *kavanah* (focus, intent, concentration) when saying *Shema* is the fact that we should be living *al kiddush Hashem*, i.e. sanctifying Hashem's Name in everything we do and at all times. That includes even dying *al kiddush Hashem* if, G-d forbid, this ever becomes necessary. Chazal tells us (Berachot 61b) that when Rabbi Akiva was being tortured by the Romans, he realised that even in that situation he was serving Hashem. He said *Shema* and declared that he had been waiting all his life for this moment, when he could fulfil the mitzvah of loving Hashem *bechol nafshecha* – "with all your soul". This means that a person must love Hashem even if He takes away his soul. Even prior to this, Rabbi Akiva's commitment to the Torah was so great that he continued teaching Torah despite threats of arrest and death, (which eventually materialised).

At the time of his death, he recited the entire *Shema* and repeated the first verse at the end. He died straight after saying the word *echad*.

The Vilna Gaon writes that the words *Shema* and *Echad* are made up of the initials of *tzaddikim* who were ready to give up their lives *al kiddush Hashem*.

Sh: Shmaryahu

M: Mishael

A (ayin): Azaria

E (alef): Avraham

Ch: Chanania

D: Daniel

Each of these *tzaddikim* was ready to die *al kiddush Hashem* in his particular predicament. However, they all survived and lived *al kiddush Hashem* for much longer.

Avraham was thrown into a furnace in Ur Kasdim for refusing to bow down to the fire-god at the command of Nimrod, but miraculously survived. This is not mentioned explicitly in the Torah, but it is hinted to in the verse (Bereishit 15:7) "I am Hashem Who took you out of Ur Kasdim". The story is related in the Midrash (Bereishit Rabbah 38:13). Avraham was relatively young at the time, and he eventually lived to the ripe old age of 175.

Chanania, Mishael and Azaria were thrown into a furnace in Babylon for refusing to bow down to an idol at the command of Nebuchadnezzar. Miraculously, they all survived. This story is related in the Book of Daniel, chapter 3. There are different opinions in the Gemara (Sanhedrin 93a) as to what happened to them afterwards. Some hold that they died shortly afterwards, while others hold that they moved to Eretz Yisrael, got married and had children.

Daniel was thrown into a lion's den for praying to Hashem against the command of King Daryavesh (Darius), but miraculously survived. This is related in chapter 6 of the Book of Daniel. According to one opinion in the Gemara (Megillah 15a), Daniel was the same person as Hatach, who delivered messages from Esther to Mordechai (Esther Chapter 4). According to the Targum on Esther 4:12, Haman executed him because he was unhappy about the messages he was delivering. Some commentators, such as Ibn Ezra, hold that the view that Daniel was Hatach is a minority opinion, and Daniel actually died of old age long before that episode.

We know almost nothing about Shmaryahu or the circumstances in which he gave up his life *al kiddush Hashem*. He lived in a generation when non-Jews outlawed Torah on the penalty of death. He was saved from death and remained loyal to Hashem and His Torah.

This combination of both living and potentially dying *al kiddush Hashem* is an exalted *kavanah* to have in mind before going to sleep.

When we feel tired and go to sleep at the end of the day, we do not want to become disconnected from Hashem. The *yetzer hara* wants to distance us from Hashem, but we counteract it by saying *Shema* before going to bed. We thereby maintain a close bond with Hashem.

We want to live *al kiddush Hashem* 24 hours a day, seven days a week!

CHAPTER 4: VIYHI NOAM

"May the pleasantness of Hashem our G-d be upon us, and may He establish the work of our hands for us, and may He establish the work of our hands."

This verse comes from Tehillim 90:17. It is the last verse of the psalm. Psalm 90 is the only psalm that is clearly attributed to Moshe Rabbenu, as it says in verse 1: "A prayer by Moshe, the man of G-d". The Torah says in *Parashat Pekudei* (Shemot 39:43) that when the *Mishkan* (tabernacle) was complete, Moshe blessed the *B'nei Yisrael*. Rashi explains, based on Chazal, that Moshe said, "May the *Shechina* rest on your handiwork", and then recited this verse (*viyhi noam*).

(The following section about *yedidut* is an original explanation by Rabbi Yerachmiel Goldman).

The word *'yadenu'* (our hands) appears twice in this verse. Through the *Mishkan*, a relationship is created between *Klal Yisrael* and Hashem as well as between each individual and Hashem.

Hand in hand (*yedidut*) refers to a closeness, a friendship, or a beloved relationship. Hand in hand with Hashem means reaching out to Hashem, building a closeness with Him (*devekut*).

The *Mishkan* was a remedy for the greatest sin the *B'nei Yisrael* had committed, i.e. the making of the golden calf.

In *Parashat Ki Tissa*, Moshe held the two tablets in his hands and then threw them down with his hands and smashed them. At that moment, *Klal Yisrael* lost its *yedidut* with Hashem.

Chazal describe the *luchot* (tablets) as being transmitted from Hashem's hands to Moshe's hands.

The only time the word '*yedid*' appears in the Torah is in *Parashat Vezot Haberacha* (Devarim 33:13). The Torah tells us that the most beloved abode of Hashem, the *Bet Hamikdash*, will be securely established in the land of the Tribe of Binyamin.

The Gemara in Menachot (53a-b) says that certain precious people and things are called *yedid*. One of these is the *Bet Hamikdash*. A person experienced *yedidut* with Hashem when walking in the *Bet Hamikdash*.

There are some pivotal moments in the Torah where the term *yad*, or a derivative of it, is mentioned twice. Examples of this are:

1) At the time of the *Akeidah* (Bereishit 22:10,12), it states, "And he stretched out his hand to slaughter the youth" and later, "Do not stretch out your hand".
2) When Yaakov received the *beracha* from Yitzchak, it states (ibid. 27:23-24), "The hands are the hands of Esav" and later, "His hands were like Esav's hands".
3) When the Jewish people were rescued at the *Yam Suf* (Sea of Reeds), it states (Shemot 14:26-27), "Stretch out your hand to the sea" and later, "And Moshe stretched out his hand".
4) When Moshe handed over the leadership to Yehoshua, it states, (Bamidbar 27:23) "And Moshe rested his hands on him, and later, "As Hashem spoke by the hand of Moshe".

All these instances refer to a closeness, a special and precious relationship. That is what the Torah is all about, being *yad beyad*, hand in hand with Hashem.

Prayer is by definition an expression of *yedidut*.

In the first blessing after *Shema* during Maariv, the word *yad* is used twice. At the beginning, it states that we are saved from the hand of kings (*yad melachim*), and at the end, it says that Yaakov was rescued from a hand stronger than him (*yad chazak mimenu*).

Towards the end of the prayer *Baruch Hashem l'olam,* (which Ashkenazim outside *Eretz Yisrael* recite in Maariv before the Amidah), the word *yad* appears three times (*yadecha, yado, yadecha*), again indicating the infinite connection to Hashem.

The Amidah itself is an expression of *yedidut* throughout.

Shabbat is replete with expressions of *yedidut*. One only has to refer to the *zemirot "Mah Yedidut"* and *"Yedid Nefesh"*, and the prayers *"Lecha Dodi", "Adon Olam"*, etc.

CHAPTER 5: YOSHEV BE'SETER ELYON (PSALM 91)

This psalm is said every Shabbat morning. It is also said most weeks on Motzei Shabbat, as well as every night as part of the Bedtime Shema.

The theme of this psalm is that Hashem protects us from the various dangers listed. We should not fear the dangers of both day and night. Hashem is the best fortress to protect us.

The Gemara (Shavuot 15b) describes this psalm as *shir shel pegaim* (a protection against tragedies) and a *shir shel negaim* (a protection against plagues).

At the beginning of the psalm, Hashem is called "Sha-ddai". One meaning of this name is that when Hashem originally created the world, it kept on expanding until He said "Enough!" (*dai*). Another meaning is that there is enough G-dliness available for every creature.

Vetachat kenafav techseh – And beneath His wings you shall take shelter. The "wings" (*kenafav*) symbolise the protective presence of the Shechinah. The Torah (Devarim 32:11) compares Hashem's protection to an eagle that hovers over its nest before landing in order not to frighten the chicks. Rashi explains that the eagle is not hunted by any other bird. Therefore, unlike other birds that carry their chicks underneath them to protect them from the eagle that soars above them, the eagle carries its chicks on its back to protect them from hunters on the ground.

Yipol mitzidecha elef urevavah miyminecha - Let a thousand fall to your side and a myriad to your right. Most commentators understand this to mean that even though large numbers of people fall in battle on all sides, Hashem will protect us. Rashi, however, interprets the word *yipol* as "camp" rather than "fall". Based on this translation, the verse can can be interpreted as saying that we have 1,000 soldiers camped on our left and 10,000 soldiers on our right (as protection). The latter ones are stronger and more important. Alternatively, they could be greater *tzaddikim* than the first ones. However, Rashi does not understand the verse to refer to soldiers but to demons. Although we are surrounded by camps of demons, Hashem protects us from them.

Elecha lo yigash - You will not be harmed. With Hashem's protection, we are invulnerable, and dangers cannot reach us. We are safe both from smaller problems and from greater ones.

Some of the words used for physical dangers (arrow, pestilence, etc) listed in this psalm are also names of demons that want to harm us by day and by night. Hashem will protect us from them.

The 1,000 and 10,000 could also refer to harmful spiritual forces that surround us, but will not harm the person who says this prayer. In a broader sense, someone who recites this psalm with the right *kavanah* has the power to protect his entire community, his family, friends, neighbours, etc. By extension, the entire *Klal Yisrael* is protected in the merit of those who recite this *tefilah*.

Ki yada shemi - For he knows My Name. The commentators explain that "knowing Hashem's Name" refers to having awareness and fear of Hashem and His Name. Hashem is with such a person and protects him.

It is an awesome realisation that anyone in his own bedroom, being in a personal, vulnerable, intimate situation, can protect himself and all of *Klal Yisrael* from dangers, tragedies and plagues by reciting this psalm.

The individual and the collective community will thereby be safe.

An interesting concluding point is that there are two traditions about how much of the psalm to say before going to bed. Some people say the entire psalm, while others will stop at the word *Machsi* ("my shelter") in the middle of verse 9, which is exactly sixty words into the psalm.

The significance of the number sixty will be explained in Chapter 13.

CHAPTER 6: MA RABU TZARAI (PSALM 3)

Verse 6 of Psalm 3 says, "I lay down and slept, yet I awoke because Hashem supports me". This makes this psalm particularly suitable for the Bedtime Shema.

The background to this psalm is that King David was running away from his son Avshalom, who wanted to take over the kingship. The story of Avshalom's rebellion appears in Shmuel Bet (Samuel II), chapters 15-18. Avshalom wanted to kill David, but David's general Yoav eventually killed Avshalom against David's explicit instructions. Through Divine inspiration, David knew he would remain king.

The psalm begins with the difficulties David is facing. David states that he has faith in Hashem, and describes Him as his shield. He prays to Hashem for protection and Hashem answers his request. David can now go to sleep and no longer needs to worry about the danger facing him.

Throughout the psalm, Avshalom is pursuing David. However, amidst all the difficulties he is experiencing, David transcends his worries and becomes aware of the larger picture. He has no worries and he is not afraid, as he trusts that salvation will come from Hashem. David blesses Hashem in a proactive way.

(The following is an original explanation by Rabbi Shmuel Brazil, Rosh Yeshiva of Zeev Hatorah, Jerusalem).

Rabbim omrim lenafshi... – Important people say to my soul that there is no salvation from G-d.

The word rabbim, important people, can refer to the four exiles:

R - Rome/Edom, i.e. the current exile

B - Bavel, the Babylonian exile

I - Yavan, Greece

M - Maddai/Paras, the Persian/Median exile

The powerful rulers of these exiles often claimed that the Jewish people would not be saved by Hashem. However, they were mistaken. Their kingdoms disappeared, and the Jewish people are still around.

Lo ira merivevot am - I do not fear the myriads of people. This can refer to the myriads of *mazikim,* harmful spiritual forces.

The conclusion is that the problems are over for now. Therefore, we can go to sleep peacefully and awake renewed with energy to deal with the issues and challenges of the day.

CHAPTER 7: HASHKIVENU

Hashkivenu is a repetition from Maariv. The prayers *Baruch Hashem l'olam, Baruch Hashem bayom* and *Yiru einenu* are also a repetition from Maariv for those who customarily recite them prior to the Maariv *Amidah*. They contain elements of compassion, closeness to Hashem and sanctification of His Name. We have to keep these ideas in mind before going to sleep.

Some versions of the Bedtime Shema do not contain *Hashkivenu* at all. Others contain both the weekday version and the version said on Shabbat/Yom Tov.

This prayer is a personal and private conversation with Hashem. In this entire paragraph, we talk directly to Hashem. For example, it says *Hashkivenu* – "Lay us down to sleep", and *Hashem Elokenu* – "Hashem our G-d".

During the plague of *Makat Bechorot* – The Smiting of the Firstborn, Hashem killed the Egyptian firstborn, but spared the Jewish firstborn. The Jewish people were very scared that night and prayed that Hashem would spare them and protect them.

Rabbeinu Yonah (Berachot 2b) writes that the Sages instituted the blessing *Hashkivenu* to commemorate the prayers that the *B'nei Yisrael* said that night. We pray that Hashem will protect us from all harm.

The Torah (Shemot 12:42) refers to Pesach night as *Leil Shimurim* (the night of guarding). For this reason, it is considered the safest night of the year. It is therefore sufficient to say only Shema and *Hamapil* before going to sleep that night.

Hashkivenu – Lay us down to sleep. We may decide when to go to bed but we are not in control of when we fall asleep. Some people have trouble falling asleep. Sometimes, this is due to disturbing thoughts, but at other times, it can happen for no obvious reason. It is therefore a blessing to fall asleep quickly. When we recite *Hashkivenu,* we are asking Hashem for this blessing.

Vehaamidenu Malkenu lechaim (tovim uleshalom) – Cause us to wake up, our King, for (good) life (and peace). In the morning, we either wake up by ourselves or with an alarm clock. We pray that we will wake up in peace, safe and sound, as sleep is a sixtieth of death. *Chaim* (life) means more than just being alive. It includes planning for the next day in *ruchniyut* (spirituality), i.e. mitzvot, Torah, *ma'asim tovim*, etc.

Vetakenenu b'eitsa tova milefanecha – Establish us in good advice before You. When you need good advice, you should speak to and pray to Hashem. With the right *kavanah,* that proper advice comes from Hashem and not from other means, such as Google. A person will therefore be more inclined to make the right decision.

A person sleeps peacefully and his soul is at rest when the day's problems have been solved and the day's work has been done. Hashem will shield us and save us from a whole range of problems, as listed in the psalm.

Vehaser Satan milefaneinu ume'achareinu – Remove impediment from in front of us and from behind us. This refers to a spiritual impediment or stumbling block. It is a broad category that can include the evil inclination (*yetzer hara*), which is synonymous with the Angel of Death (*malach hamavet*).

Lefanenu refers to impediments that are right presently there, or heading towards the future.

Achareinu refers to impediments that originated in the past. Sometimes, they are hidden and the person is unaware that they pursue him.

Ki Kel Shomereinu umatzilenu Atah – For You are G-d, our Guardian and our Saviour.

Shomreinu, Hashem protects us from problems before they even arise.

Matzilenu, Hashem saves us from problems that have already happened.

Baruch Hashem bayom ... - Blessed is Hashem in the day, blessed is Hashem in the night. This sentence seems to be in the wrong order. Night should be mentioned before day, just as the prayer mentions going to bed before getting up. However, the meaning is not literally day and night but brightness versus gloom and clear times in life versus dark times. In essence, this prayer is teaching us that we have to see Hashem's blessings even in difficult times. Day is mentioned first because Hashem's blessings are more obvious during the bright times of life. However, if we think into the matter properly, we will also appreciate Hashem's blessings during the most difficult parts of life.

The word *'yad'* appears three times in this prayer, which makes it a *chazaka*. (When something occurs three times, it is classified as a *chazaka,* meaning something that is firmly established.) Here, our *yedidut*, endearment and closeness to Hashem, is confirmed. We are, so to speak, holding hands with Hashem, or shaking hands with Him.

Yiru einenu – May our eyes see. This paragraph refers to the coming of Mashiach and the rebuilding of the *Bet Hamikdash*.

Hashem Melech - Hashem is, was and always will be King. There is no other king.

Again, the language here is personal, allowing us to experience feelings of closeness to Hashem.

CHAPTER 8: HAMALACH HAGOEL

"May the angel that redeems me from all bad, bless the youths, and may my name be called upon them, and the names of my fathers Avraham and Yitzchak, and may they proliferate like fish in the midst of the land".

This verse comes from Parashat Vayechi (Bereishit 48:16) and was said by Yaakov on his deathbed at the age of 147. It is not a prayer to an angel, but is a prayer to Hashem, who regularly sent an angel to protect Yaakov.

Yaakov said this verse while blessing his grandchildren Menashe and Ephraim, Yosef's sons. He crossed his arms and put his right hand on Ephraim's head, even though he was the younger brother. Yaakov foresaw that he and his descendants would be greater than Menashe and his descendants.

The Torah introduces this verse by saying that Yaakov blessed Yosef. At face value, this seems strange, as the blessing is directed to Ephraim and Menashe. We therefore understand from here that the best blessing to give a father is a blessing for his children.

The beginning of the verse (*hamalach hago'el oti mikol ra* – "the angel that redeems me from all bad") is in the present tense. Yaakov was saying that the angel was actively redeeming him at that time. This seems quite ironic as Yaakov is on his deathbed. How can the angel be redeeming him "from all bad" if he is about to die? Is death not considered "bad"?

The answer is that for Yaakov, death was not '*ra*' (bad) or even scary. It was merely the means for him to go to the place of eternal reward.

The experience or process of death is different for everyone, depending on the connection between body and soul. Death is a difficult experience when a person's soul is intertwined with his body. This is the case with people who have a greater connection with the material aspect of the world. *Tzaddikim*, righteous people, have a pure soul, that is completely detached from materialism. Therefore, they find the process of death easier to cope with.

The Gemara in Taanit (5b) says that Yaakov did not die. Indeed, his name lives on because the Jewish people are called the "Children of Israel". (Israel is Yaakov, as Hashem changed Yaakov's name to Yisrael). Yaakov Avinu lives on through his children and descendants until this day.

There are three ways of understanding the meaning of *hamalach*, the angel.

According to Rashi, the angel referred to here is an actual angel. Of course, it is not independent of Hashem, but is a messenger whom Hashem sent to give over His blessing.

The Ohr Hachaim explains that the "angel" referred to here is the Word of Hashem to His beloved prophets. Hashem's Word is sometimes described as an angel because when Hashem speaks, angels are being created. According to this, *Hamalach Hagoel* does not refer to an angel, but to Hashem Himself. Yaakov was saying that Hashem's Word should help and bless Ephraim and Menashe.

Finally, the *Zohar* (Mishpatim) refers to the Divine presence (Shechinah) as an angel that accompanies a person everywhere he goes, as long as he keeps the Torah and mitzvot.

In *Tefilat Haderech* (the wayfarer's prayer), we read a verse that refers to Yaakov's encounter with angels (Bereishit 32:2-3). Yaakov met angels of Hashem on his way back home from

Lavan's house. Rashi explains that these were the angels of Eretz Yisrael that came to protect him when he returned there.

Veyidgu larov – May they proliferate like fish. Fish live under water, shielded from the evil eye. For this reason, the *Mishnah Berurah* (583:8) advises people to recite Tashlich on Rosh Hashanah next to a body of water that contains fish. This is an auspicious act, as we express our hope that the evil eye will have no power over us just as it has no power over fish. Additionally, we pray that just as fish multiply in abundance, so should we.

The Torah is compared to water. Just as fish require water to survive, so do the Jewish people need Torah in order to survive (Berachot 61b).

Bekerev Ha'aretz - In the midst of the land. This refers to the Land of Israel, where real growth happens. All the tribes began to multiply when they entered the Land of Israel.

CHAPTER 9: IM SHAMOA TISHMA

"If you listen to the voice of Hashem your G-d, and do what is correct in His eyes, and you listen to his mitzvot, all the illnesses that I placed upon Egypt I will not place upon you, as I am Hashem your healer".

This *passuk* comes from *Parashat Beshalach*, Shemot 15:26. It is read on the seventh day of Pesach. The Torah describes how the *B'nei Yisrael* encountered bitter waters during their travels in the wilderness following the splitting of the Sea of Reeds. The water was too bitter for the people to drink, so the people complained to Moshe, asking him what they are going to drink. Hashem showed Moshe some wood, which he threw into the water. The water became sweet and the people drank it.

This *passuk* is the last *passuk* of the section of the bitter waters, which concludes the Torah reading of the seventh day of Pesach.

The Gemara in Berachot 5a says that suffering runs away from anybody who learns Torah. One of the sources mentioned there is this *passuk*. It is therefore very fitting to say this *passuk* at bedtime when we pray to be saved from the perils of the night.

The Midrash Tehillim writes that if we have a strong desire for Hashem to listen to our prayers, then we have to listen to Hashem.

The Gemara (Berachot 40a) says that in the physical realm, you can put whatever you want in an empty vessel until it is full, and there is then no space for anything anymore.

This is in stark contrast to spiritual matters. When a person is full of Torah knowledge, there is always room for more, but it is very difficult to put such knowledge into a person who lacks Torah knowledge.

The Mechilta writes that this *passuk* refers to the entire Torah:

Kol Hashem – The voice of Hashem. This refers to to the Ten Commandments, which were given directly from Hashem to the *B'nei Yisrael*.

Vehayashar – That which is correct. This refers to *aggadeta* (non-halachic parts of the Oral Torah, such as stories, parables and lessons).

Veha'azanta – You will listen. This refers to *halachot* and *gezeirot* (Rabbinic decrees).

Veshamarta – You will guard. This refers to the prohibition of inappropriate relationships.

Hamachala…ki ani Hashem rof'echa – The illness…for I am Hashem your healer. This implies that Hashem is the healer for the World to Come.

That is, if someone abides by this *passuk*, he will be healed in *Olam Haba*.

Listening to the voice of Hashem can also mean that we need to have respect for *talmidei chachamim*. When we listen to *divrei Torah,* it is as if we are standing before Hashem.

Even business should be conducted with *emunah* (integrity, loyalty to Hashem). Every time one does business with integrity, it is as if one kept the whole Torah (Mechilta ibid.).

CHAPTER 10: VAYOMER HASHEM EL HASATAN - DENOUNCING THE SATAN

"And Hashem said to the Satan, "Hashem will denounce you, Satan! Hashem, who chooses Jerusalem, will denounce you! Surely he (Yehoshua the High Priest) is a firebrand removed from fire" (Zechariah 3:2).

In Ashkenazi communities, the Chazan recites part of this *passuk* before Mussaf on Rosh Hashanah and Yom Kippur as a prayer that Hashem will denounce the Satan and not allow it to impede him or his prayer.

The Satan is more overt and rampant in the evening and night. This is why we need protection at that time. Nighttime is a metaphor for *galut*, exile. By denouncing the Satan, Hashem will save us from being harmed by other nations during the exile.

The Satan, the evil inclination (*yetzer hara*) and the Angel to Death (*malach hamavet*) are all the same entity (Gemara Bava Batra 16a).

At the end of the Babylonian exile, the Satan had come to accuse the High Priest Yehoshua for not protesting against his sons, who had married non-Jewish women. Hashem, who had chosen Jerusalem, denounced the Satan, saying that Yehoshua had been saved from Nebuchadnezzar when he threw him into a fire together with some false prophets. This demonstrated that he had great merits and did not deserve to be accused by Satan (Sanhedrin 93a, Metzudat David on Zechariah 3:1-2).

By extension, in every generation, K'lal Yisrael are likened to a firebrand saved from fire.

When we say this *passuk* before going to bed, it is similar to reciting the Musaf prayer. This is because there are two aspects to the protection Hashem provided for Yehoshua the High Priest. Firstly, we see that Hashem is merciful, and secondly, that He chose Jerusalem as the location of the Temple and its service. Malbim explains that since Yehoshua's ancestors served in the First Temple in Jerusalem, the merit of this holy place provided Yehoshua with miraculous protection.

The significance of Jerusalem is not limited to the High Priest. We pray daily for the rebuilding of Jerusalem (in the *Amidah* and *Birkat Hamazon*).

The Gemara in Berachot 51a says that the Angel of Death accompanies women on their way back from a funeral. Maharsha explains that this is because Chavah, the first woman, brought death to the world by eating from the fruit of the Tree of Knowledge and influencing Adam to eat from it. At a funeral, a time of Divine wrath, the Angel of Death accompanies them. Therefore, if someone is walking along the road and meets them, and has no other way to go, he should recite this *passuk* as a *segula* to be saved from the Angel to Death.

It could be suggested that since sleep is a sixtieth of death, we recite this *passuk* before going to sleep to protect us from any harm.

We already mentioned that the Satan, *yetzer hara* and *malach hamavet* are all the same angel. However, the various terms refer to the different ways in which he appears.

The term Satan is used when the angel brings about negative consequences to a person from without.

At the time of the *Akeidah*, the Satan revealed to Sarah that Abraham was going to sacrifice Yitzchak. Sarah was so shocked to hear this that she died (Midrash Tanchuma, Vayeira 23). At a later stage, the Satan brought confusion to the world, which led to Jewish people making the golden calf (Gemara Shabbat 89a).

The Satan is therefore a messenger, an agent who comes to test us. When a person makes the right decision, he can remove the Satan. Once he chooses not to sin, Hashem assists him by removing temptation. When this occurs, the *yetzer hara* is turned into the *yetzer hatov*. The evil inclination becomes a good inclination.

The Gemara in Sukkah 52a states that when Hashem destroys the *Yetzer Hara*, both the righteous and the wicked will cry. The righteous will see the *Yetzer Hara* in the form of a tall mountain, and will cry in amazement that they were able to overcome it. The wicked will see it as a single strand of hair, and will cry because they were unable to overcome something as insignificant as a hair. We learn from here that the battle against the Satan is simple yet difficult.

CHAPTER 11: HINEI MITATO SHELISHLOMO SHISHIM GIBORIM - SIXTY WARRIORS

"Behold, the bed of Shlomo! Sixty mighty warriors are around it from the mighty warriors of Israel. They all hold swords and are experienced in battle. Each has his sword by his thigh (to protect him) from the fear of night." (Shir Hashirim [Song of Songs] 3:7-8)

In some *siddurim*, these verses are prefaced by two verses from psalm 149:5-6.

Shlomo Hamelech and his warriors were afraid of the night. These verses are very fitting for the Bedtime Shema, as they contain words of Torah and are clearly referring to the dangers of the night and the need for protection.

The Toldos Aharon quotes four Gemarot that discuss these verses:

Shavuot 35b

Yevamot 109b

Gittin 68b

Sanhedrin 20b

In Shavuot, it states that whenever Shlomo is mentioned in Shir Hashirim (except 8:12), it refers to Hashem, who is the King to Whom all peace belongs - *Melech sh'hashalom shelo*. Some say that these verses are an exception to this, as where the bed of

Shlomo is mentioned, it does not refer to Hashem, but to Shlomo himself.

In Yevamot, it says that a judge should always have in mind that there is a sword between his thighs and *Gehinnom* is open beneath him (where he may fall if he judges wrongly). The source brought for this teaching is our *passuk,* as "night" also refers to *Gehinnom.* Rashi explains that the *gibborim* (mighty warriors) referred to in the *passuk* are the *dayanim* (judges).

In Gittin, the story is told of Ashmidai, the demon king, who was engaged in a battle against Shlomo. Eventually, Shlomo captured Ashmidai. Shlomo had a necklace and ring with Hashem's name on it that kept his prisoner in check.

However, Ashmidai managed to free himself. He swallowed Shlomo and threw him 400 parsot (over 1000 miles) away.

Ashmidai took on a likeness of Shlomo and sat on his throne as an imposter.

Meanwhile, Shlomo was suffering and going around begging. When he came before the Sanhedrin and identified himself, the Rabbis became suspicious of the man sitting on the throne. They realised the sitting king was an imposter after finding out that he was visiting the queens at night while they were *niddah*.

The Sages gave Shlomo the necklace and ring with Hashem's name. Just in time, Ashmidai flew away and escaped.

Shlomo remained scared that Ashmidai would return, so surrounded himself with sixty warriors for protection.

Several sources (R' Avraham Pelagi, Arizal, Beis Halevi) point out that *mazikim* (destructive spirits) really exist. These pesukim shield us from things that we do not see.

In Sanhedrin, the reference is similar to that in Gittin. If refers to the different stages that Shlomo lost his kingdom to the demon Ashmidai. At one stage, he was only king over his bed. Our *passuk* refers to this stage.

Rashi on Shir Hashirim understands "Shlomo" in these verses to refer to Hashem. He explains that the "bed" refers to the *Mishkan* and the "sixty warriors" refers to the 600,000 Jews in the *midbar* (wilderness). The "experience in battle" mentioned here means Torah scholars, who are experienced in Torah discussions, as well as *Kohanim,* who are experienced in the Divine service. The "swords" are the teachings and traditions that prevent the Torah from being forgotten. Finally, the "fear of the night" refers to the fear that they might forget the Torah.

The Netziv says that "sixty warriors" is a reference to the sixty tractates of the Talmud. Every Jew is a warrior in the battle for the truth of the Torah.

It says in the *Zohar Chadash* (Shir Hashirim 661) that there are 600,000 letters in a Sefer Torah and every Jew corresponds to a letter. (As there are actually 304,805 letters in the Torah, this statement is probably meant to be understood in a metaphorical sense).

Seforno explains that the fear of the night is a reference to the night of Tisha B'Av.

The Alshich says that we should not compare ourselves to the generation who dwelled in the *midbar*. They were so much greater than we are. When 600,000 men said *na'aseh venishma* (we will do and then we will understand) on Mount Sinai, they each created an angel. 600,000 angels were thus created.

Although the Mishnah in Pirkei Avot says that every mitzvah that we perform creates an angel, we are not on the same spiritual level as the generation of the *midbar*.

The bed is a private and intimate place. The sword by the thigh refers to the *brit milah* between the thighs. The fear of the night means that one should pray to have proper dreams and guard the *kedusha* of the *brit milah*.

The Jewish bed is compared to the *Mishkan*. Hashem is there with the husband and wife, and their *shalom bayit* maintains the *kedusha* of the bed and the home.

The bed is therefore a holy place where upon waking up we say *Modeh Ani*.

CHAPTER 12: BIRKAT KOHANIM

"May Hashem bless you and guard you. May Hashem illuminate His Face towards you and be gracious to you. May Hashem lift His Face to you and grant you peace." (Bamidbar 6:24-26)

In most communities in Eretz Yisrael, and in some Sephardi communities worldwide, the Kohanim recite *Birkat Kohanim* (priestly blessing) every Shacharit and every Mussaf. In some communities in the Galilee, it is only said in Mussaf. In Ashkenazi communities in the Diaspora, it is only said in Mussaf of Yom Tov. We also say it every morning following the *berachot* on the Torah, and on Friday night when we bless our children.

There is a lot to say about *Birkat Kohanim*. In this chapter, we will limit ourselves to relevant points.

During the Bedtime Shema, we say this blessing while alone. We say it to Hashem, but for ourselves. This blessing is formulated in the singular. This means that it is a blessing from Hashem for each individual.

According to Rashi on these verses, the first verse is a blessing for physical prosperity and safety. *Yevarechecha* is a blessing for money, property and possessions, while *yishmerecha* is a protection against thieves and plunderers. There is no point of being blessed with physical possessions if thieves steal them. Hashem not only provides the possessions, but He also guards them from being stolen or damaged. This blessing is particularly relevant in the night, the time when thieves tend to operate.

In the second verse, we ask Hashem to give us grace and shine His countenance on us. This implies unity and closeness with Hashem, which is what we want at night. We need a light in the darkness.

In the third verse, we make a request for peace, which is the ultimate blessing.

This fits in very well with the general theme of the Bedtime Shema, which is that we say words of Torah before going to sleep and ask Hashem for protection during the night.

There are several connections between *Birkat Kohanim* and the sixty warriors discussed in the previous chapter.

Chazal tell us (Midrash Shir Hashirim Rabbah 3) that the sixty warriors that protect us at night are actually the sixty letters of *Birkat Kohanim*.

Ramchal links this blessing to Psalm 121, which is described in more detail Chapter 14. It says there, "*Hineh lo yanum* … Hashem, Who protects Israel, neither slumbers nor sleeps". The *gematria* of the word *Hineh* is 60 (=5 + 50 + 5).

At night, the name Elokim rules, which is the *middah* of *din* (attribute of strict judgement). The sixty letters and warriors break through the darkness of the night to protect us from the dangers that could come about through this attribute.

The Kli Yakar (on the verses of *Birkat Kohanim*) explains that since the letter yud is spelled yud, vav, daled, it can be considered to have a *gematria* of 20 (=10 + 6 + 4). As the three verses of this blessing each start with yud, we come to a total of 60. This corresponds to the sixty letters of *birkat Kohanim*, which are compared to sixty mighty warriors.

Furthermore, he explains that Chazal tell us (Gemara Niddah 31a) that there are three partners in the creation of a person - Hashem, the father and the mother.

The father contributes five white elements: bones, sinews, nails, the brain and the white of the eye.

The mother contributes five red elements: skin, blood, flesh, hair, and the dark part of the eye.

Hashem contributes ten spiritual elements: the *ruach,* the *neshama,* walking, talking, seeing, hearing, the form of the face, wisdom, knowledge and intellect.

The ten fingers of the Kohanim are the conduit through which the ten revealed physical blessings are provided, as well as the ten hidden spiritual blessings.

With this in mind, when saying the Bedtime Shema, there is the potential to pray to have children and/or a blessing for our children.

CHAPTER 13: REFLECTIONS ON THE NUMBER SIXTY

In Chapter 5, we discussed Psalm 91, *Yoshev beseter Elyon*. Although some people recite the entire psalm, others have the custom of only reciting the first sixty words, stopping at *machsi* in verse 9.

In Chapter 10, we discussed the sixty warriors surrounding Shlomo's bed.

Finally, in Chapter 11, we expounded on the priestly blessing and explained the link to the number sixty, including the fact that the blessing contains sixty letters.

The number sixty is often used by Chazal to mean "many". When used in the context of a blessing, it means that the blessing should be fulfilled in abundance and in a multi-faceted and inclusive way.

Rabbeinu Bachya brings a Midrash, which discusses the passuk in Shir Hashirim about sixty warriors surrounding Shlomo's bed. Did King Solomon require protection of this sort? Rather, it refers to the sixty letters of *Birkat Kohanim*, which were inscribed around his bed. It was these letters that protected him from harm.

The reason why some people have the custom to only recite the first sixty words of Psalm 91 before going to bed is to invoke the merit of the sixty letters of *Birkat Kohanim*, in the same way as Shlomo Hamelech had the words of these blessings inscribed around his bed. Those who follow this custom are of the opinion that invoking this merit outweighs the benefit of reciting the entire psalm.

(The following explanation of the number sixty is based on the teachings of Rabbi Moshe Shapiro.)

The significance of the number sixty is that it is the smallest portion of something to be considered significant. We find this principle in the law that if non-kosher food was inadvertently mixed into kosher food, as long as the proportion of non-kosher food is less than one in sixty (battel beshishim), it is permitted to eat the mixture (Shulchan Aruch Yoreh De'ah 98:1).

Since a sixtieth is the smallest proportion to be significant, Chazal (Gemara Berachot 57b) used the term "one in sixty" to refer to something that provides a slight taste or experience of something greater. These things contain one or more features of the greater thing that they are compared to. They give five examples of this: fire is a sixtieth of *Gehinnom*, honey is a sixtieth of *manna*, Shabbat is a sixtieth of the World to Come, sleep is a sixtieth of death, and a dream is a sixtieth of prophecy. Based on the teaching that sleep is a sixtieth of death, we say in Hamapil, "Veha'er einai pen ishan hamavet" – "Enlighten my eyes lest I sleep the sleep of death". Later sources say that choosing a name for a child is a sixtieth of Divine inspiration.

We also see this principle from various laws discussed by the Rambam. The Rambam tells us (Bikkurim 2:17) that although the Torah does not require a specific amount to be separated for *Bikkurim* (first fruits), the Rabbis decreed that the minimum amount that a person should separate is a sixtieth. Additionally, he tells us (Terumah 3:1-2) that the Rabbis instituted that a person may not give less than a sixtieth of his produce as *Terumah* (the portion separated for the Kohen).

Baal Haturim finds a hint in the Torah (Devarim 26:5) that *Bikkurim* should not be less than a sixtieth. When the Torah refers to the basket used for *Bikkurim*, it calls it a *teneh* (instead of the more common word *sal*). This word has the gematria of 60, which hints to the Rabbinic decree that the minimum amount to separate for *Bikkurim* is a sixtieth. Another hint to this is the fact that the only letter that does not appear in the parashah of *Bikkurim* is the letter *samech*, which has the numerical value of sixty.

CHAPTER 14: HINEI LO YANUM - OUR GUARDIAN DOES NOT SLUMBER OR SLEEP

"Behold! The Guardian of Israel does not slumber or sleep" (Tehillim 121:4).

This verse comes from Psalm 121 and was briefly discussed in Chapter 11.

Some people repeat this verse three times. Others recite the whole of Psalm 121.

This verse contains a double declaration that Hashem does not sleep. In none of our prayers do we mention Hashem having the need to eat or having other physical needs. This is obvious, as Hashem is not human, does not have a body and is not physical. Hashem is completely detached from physical matters and does not have any needs whatsoever. This raises the question as to why we need to say that Hashem does not sleep. Radak explains that it is not referring to physical sleep. It means that Hashem never removes His constant supervision and protection of the Jewish people, even when they are in exile. Therefore, the Jewish people can never be destroyed. Metzudat David also explains this verse to refer to Hashem's constant supervision of the Jewish people.

We say this verse in the Bedtime Shema because it talks about sleep and Hashem guarding Israel. This is the perfect antidote to the dangers of the night. Furthermore, we thereby go to sleep with words of Torah.

Ibn Ezra says that Israel in this verse refers to Yaakov Avinu. While he slept, he had the dream of the ladder, in which Hashem promised that He would guard him wherever he went (Bereishit 28:15).

When we sleep, we are returning our souls to their source in Heaven in order to be refreshed. This is the only psalm that starts with *Shir lamaalot* rather than *Shir hamaalot*. Rashi explains that this refers to the high level that the righteous will attain in the World to Come. *Shir hamaalot* does not refer to such a high level.

Radak says that when we are in exile, it is as if we are sleeping. *Yanum* (slumber) is a lighter or lower level of sleep, while *yishan* (sleep) is a full-blown sleep.

The Gemara in Sotah 48a describes the Levi'im singing 'Arise! Why are you sleeping, Hashem?' (Tehillim 44:24). The Gemara asks that this seems to contradict our verse (that states that Hashem never sleeps). The Gemara answers that although Hashem never sleeps, He sometimes makes it appear as if He is asleep and allows the Jewish people to suffer while other nations experience pleasure and tranquillity.

There have been times when the Jewish people had great difficulties or were persecuted. At other times, they were prosperous and successful. One could have the impression that Hashem is asleep in bad times and only guards the Jewish people in good times.

Nothing could be further from the truth.

The Gemara in Megillah 13b quotes Haman saying that the Jewish people are sleeping in a spiritual sense, as they are not particular in their observance of *mitzvot*. Therefore, he claimed that Hashem would not protect them, as He separated Himself from the Jewish people and took away His personal connection with them.

Previously, during the times of Bilam and Amalek, the Jews were afraid but they knew Hashem was there protecting them. However, during the Purim episode, the Jewish people seemed doomed due to their sins, as they attended the king's banquets as well as having bowed down to Nebuchadnezzar's image some years earlier. Mordechai realised this, and advised the Jews to do *teshuvah*. The Jews listened to him, and returned to Hashem wholeheartedly during their three-day fast.

The night that King Achashverosh could not sleep and consulted his books (Esther 6:1-2) was the beginning of the reversal of the Jews' fortune. It is a metaphor for Hashem "waking up" and destroying their enemies.

During times of *hester panim* (when Hashem hides His Face), when the situation appears very bad for the Jewish people, it would seem that Hashem is asleep and not attentive.

However, we know that through *teshuvah, tefillah* and *tzedakah* (repentance, prayer and charitable donations), we can break through this slumber and cancel all harmful decrees.

CHAPTER 15: LESHUATECHA KIVITI HASHEM

"For your salvation I hope, Hashem" (Bereishit 49:18).

In some *siddurim* this verse appears in three different combinations, all of which are recited three times.

This verse is found in Parashat Vayechi and was said by Yaakov Avinu on his deathbed as a blessing to Dan.

According to Rashi, Yaakov had a prophecy about Samson's death and how he would pray for Hashem's salvation.

Other commentators, such as Midrash Rabba, Targum Yonatan and Ramban, explain that when Yaakov foresaw that Samson would destroy the Philistine temple, killing thousands of Philistines, he considered the possibility that he would be the *Mashiach*. However, when he foresaw that Samson would die in the process, he realised that he was not going to be the Messiah, as that salvation has to come from Hashem and will last forever

The prophet Eliyahu will announce the Messiah, who will come from the tribe of Yehudah and not from the tribe of Dan. This verse expresses Yaakov's longing for Hashem's true salvation through the coming of *Mashiach*.

Rabbenu Bachye says that ultimately, Yaakov was praying for Samson to be saved. Although he died, it was considered as if he was saved because he killed so many enemies of the Jewish people.

He says that those who understand the names of Hashem find in this verse a name of Hashem that allows the one who says it to overcome his enemies. This name is derived from a threefold combination of this verse.

The reason for including this verse in the Bedtime Shema is not clear; a few suggestions can be made.

The verse refers to salvation, and hints to a Divine Name that brings us salvation from our enemies. When we go to sleep, we pray to Hashem to save us from the dangers of the night.

In the morning blessings, we thank Hashem for giving sight to the blind (*pokeach ivrim*). When we sleep, we are blind and vulnerable. As Samson was blinded, we thank Hashem for allowing us to see when we wake up.

The Bedtime Shema is a recognition that we are blind and vulnerable to the dangers of the night. When we are asleep, we do not know what is going on around us.

Some of the most dramatic and heroic moments take place in private. Fearing Heaven in private is considered particularly virtuous. We can all aspire to be like Samson and bring down our enemies in a dramatic fashion. However, Judaism also recognises greatness in private moments, e.g. saying the Bedtime Shema every single day, even when one is exhausted and cannot wait to go to sleep.

Finally, this verse might refer to the ultimate redemption, the idea of yearning for *Mashiach*.

The Bedtime Shema has little or no reference to *Mashiach*, except for this verse. The verse also includes our personal salvation, including our children, our families, health, work, comforts, etc. We ask Hashem to enhance our own lives and by extension the lives of the entire Jewish people.

CHAPTER 16: BESHEM HASHEM ELOKEI YISRAEL - THE FOUR ANGELS SURROUNDING US

"In the name of Hashem G-d of Israel, may Michael be on my right, Gabriel on my left, Uriel in front of me, Raphael behind me, and upon my head the Presence of G-d".

This line is not included in all versions of the Bedtime Shema.

One of the few times we mention angels in our prayers is during Minchah on Yom Kippur (according to Ashkenazi custom). We say that Michael is on the right and Gabriel is on the left. (Sephardim mention these angels in Neilah, but do not mention the right and left).

During the Bedtime Shema, we mention four angels who protect in all four directions. Michael is on the right, Gabriel on the left, Uriel at the front and Raphael at the rear. Above our heads, on top of us, is Hashem himself. Therefore, every individual is protected by Hashem and by four of His main angels.

We say this in the Bedtime Shema because we need protection from the dangers of the night. We pray to Hashem for the blessings of safety and security.

Pirkei D'Rabbi Eliezer (Chapter 4) describes the Creation of the world. On the second day of Creation, Hashem created the firmament and the angels. When angels are sent by Hashem on a mission, they take on the form of *ruach* (wind or spirit). When they serve Hashem, they take on the form of fire.

There are four groups of ministering angels. Michael the leader of the group on the right, Gavriel is the leader of the group on the left, Uriel is the leader of the group in the front and Raphael is the leader of the group at the back. In the middle is the Throne of Glory (*kisei hakavod*) with Hashem's Presence above it. In the middle of the night, Hashem stands above us and we become the focal point. This is a great blessing for such a mundane setting as going to sleep.

The Midrash (Bamidbar Rabbah 2:10) describes how the Twelve Tribes surrounded the Mishkan in groups of three, led by an angel, each with their flag.

Michael accompanied the southern group (Reuven, Shimon, Gad). His name comes from the combination of two verses, *mi chamocha* ("Who is like You" – Shemot 15:11), which the Jewish people said when Hashem split the Yam Suf, and *ein ka'kel* ("Who is like G-d" – Devarim 33:26), which Moshe said at the conclusion of the Torah.

Uriel accompanied the northern group (Dan, Asher, Naftali). His name refers to the light of G-d that emanates from the Tanach. Through the Torah, Hashem brings atonement and light to the Jewish people. (The name Uriel comes from the word *ohr* - light).

Gabriel accompanied the eastern group (Yehuda, Yisachar, Zevulun). His name refers to Hashem's strength (*gevurah*). Yehuda was blessed with particular strength.

Raphael accompanied the western group (Ephraim, Menashe, Binyamin). The name Rafael means Hashem's healer. Moshe prayed that Miriam should be healed, *Kel na refa na la.* This prayer contains Raphael's name.

In the *midbar* (wilderness), millions of Jews were protected by these four angels. Nowadays, Hashem offers the same protection to every individual. Angels are from the spiritual world, so they are not limited by physical restraints. Therefore, each of the four angels can be with every person.

This phrase is repeated three times. When something is done three times, it becomes a *chazakah* (something fixed or well-established). In this case it becomes a *chazakah* for protection.

As an aside, as great as angels are, they have no free will. A person has the potential to reach great heights by making the right decisions. A person has more potential than an angel, as he is able to become great through his free will. The free will of a human being is greater than the robotic nature of an angel.

That is why we have to exercise this free will to say the Bedtime Shema every night!

CHAPTER 17: THE JEWISH HOME (PSALM 128)

This psalm is not found in all versions of the Bedtime Shema.

This psalm describes the Jewish home as King David envisioned it.

It mentions children around the table, which is a reference to having a family and the security that this brings.

Ashrei kol yerei Hashem haholech bidrachav - Praiseworthy are all those who fear Hashem and walk in His ways.

Rashi explains that the word *kol* (all) is used here to teach us that this applies to both men and women.

Metzudat David explains that *yerei Hashem* (those who fear Hashem) refers to being careful not to transgress the negative commandments, and *haholech bidrachav* (those who walk in His ways) refers to fulfilling the positive commandments.

Haholech bidrachav implies that we should know Hashem in all our ways. Everything we do can be transformed into a mitzvah. This includes even the most mundane things we do every day, including sleep, as long as we intend to make a connection to Hashem through all our actions.

Serving Hashem out of fear of punishment is a lower level of service. A higher level of *yirat shamayim* is called *yirat haromemut*. This means that one recognizes Hashem's infinite power and grandeur and is in awe of it. This includes admiring every part of creation. This type of fear and awe is really love of Hashem, and offers reward in this world and the next world. Fear and love are distinct feelings, but are not mutually exclusive.

When parents serve Hashem out of love, this has a major impact on their children and it is very likely that they will emulate their parents.

This psalm is a *segulah* to find a good spouse and to have children as well as to maintain these blessings if we have them.

Banecha kishtilei zeitim – Your children are like olive shoots. Jewish children are compared to olive shoots. Olive trees do not tolerate grafting. Characteristics of olive oil are that it does not mix with other liquids, it rises to the top and it gives a bright light. This comparison teaches us the importance of guarding the Jewish people against assimilation and intermarriage. This is particularly so with children, who are very impressionable.

CHAPTER 18: RIGZU V'AL TECHETA'U – TREMBLE AND DO NOT SIN

"Tremble and do not sin. Reflect in your hearts while on your beds and be silent, Selah" (Tehillim 4:5).

This verse is the source for the Bedtime Shema. The Gemara (Berachot 4b) says in the name of Rabbi Yehoshua ben Levi that even though a person recited *Shema* in Maariv, it is a mitzvah for him to repeat it when going to bed. The Gemara quotes the statement of a sage (in our texts, it refers to him as "Rabbi Yossi", but the marginal note in the Vilna Shas says that it should say "Rav Assi" or "Rav Yosef") that the source for this requirement is the above verse. Rashi explains that the phrase *imru vilvavchem* – "say in your hearts" means that you should say *Shema*, in which it states *al levavecha* – "upon your heart". *Al mishkavchem* – "on your beds" refers to the command to say Shema *beshochbecha* – "when you lie down". *Vedomu* – "and be silent" means that immediately after reciting Shema, a person should go to sleep, at which time he will be silent.

However, Rav Nachman states that a *talmid chacham* is exempt from reciting the Bedtime Shema because he constantly reviews his learning. Nevertheless, Abaye says that even a *talmid chacham* is required to say one verse asking for Divine mercy, such as *beyadecha afkid ruchi* – "In Your Hand I entrust my soul" – Tehillim 31:6, because the night is dark and dangerous.

In Parashat Balak (Bamidbar 23:24), Bilaam prophesied that the Jewish people would not go to sleep until they defeated their enemies. Rashi explains this to mean that they will destroy and devour their spiritual enemies, namely, harmful spiritual forces, by reciting the Bedtime Shema.

Bilaam was looking for weaknesses in the Jewish people so that he could curse them, but he could only find strengths. Hashem therefore transformed his curses into blessings.

In essence, the Bedtime Shema is the best remedy for sleep issues.

In Psalm 4, verses 3-6 (including our verse), King David is speaking to his enemies. Rashi explains that these are King Saul's followers, who were trying to bring about David's downfall. David was concerned that they might harm him in order to receive a reward from Saul. He asked them to trust in Hashem instead, as He will provide abundant blessing for those who are righteous and do not cause any harm.

Radak says that *Rigzu* (tremble) implies fear, and refers to fear of Hashem.

At bedtime, a person can relax and be free from the worries of the day. We should be silent and stop sinning. It is a good time for *cheshbon hanefesh* - reviewing our actions and thoughts of the day. After doing this, a person should say Bedtime Shema and go to sleep.

The Gemara in Berachot 5a says that a person should constantly arouse his good inclination to wage war against his evil inclination. We should fight the evil inclination and endeavour to beat it. If this does not work, he should learn Torah. When a person learns Torah, he is automatically fighting against the evil inclination. If that does not work, he should say Shema. If even this does not work, he should think about the day of death.

The Gemara derives this lesson from our verse. *Rigzu* (tremble) can also mean to do battle. This refers to fighting the *yetzer hara*. *Imru vilvavchem* (say with your hearts) refers to Torah study. *Al mishkavchem* (on your beds) refers to the Shema, which is said when going to bed. *Vedomu selah* (and be silent, Selah) refers to the day of death, when a person is silent forever. (One of the meanings of Selah is forever).

Chazal say that we should not take it for granted that we will sin. We should be sensitive and mindful to sin, and should stop and think before acting in order not to stumble into sin.

The Amidah contains two blessings against sinning, thereby reminding us three times a day about the importance of avoiding sin. Furthermore, when we say *'ata chonantanu'* on Motzei Shabbat, we pray that the week will be peaceful and free and clean of any sin.

Elsewhere, the question is asked whether it would have been better for a person to have been born as a righteous person or whether it is better for him to struggle with his evil inclination. The answer is that the latter is better because struggling makes one into a better person. It is perfectly fine to have struggles and questions as long as one beats the evil inclination in its proper time.

In conclusion, this verse is a reminder of the constant battle against our evil inclination.

CHAPTER 19: ADON OLAM

Some people say the entire *Adon Olam*, while others only say the final lines of the prayer, *b'yado afkid ruchi* (in His Hand I entrust my soul), which is relevant to going to sleep at night. It is said towards the end of the Bedtime Shema.

A full commentary on *Adon Olam* is beyond the scope of this chapter. After some general observations, references will be made to the link between *Adon Olam* and the Bedtime Shema.

It is not certain who wrote *Adon Olam*. Many believe that it was written by R' Shlomo ibn Gabirol. It is a declaration of the timelessness, omnipotence and power of Hashem.

It is interesting to note that we say *Adon Olam* in the morning at the beginning of Shacharit and again before going to sleep. We start and end the day with the basic and fundamental teaching of this prayer.

Reciting *Adon Olam* is an opportunity to recognise Hashem as our King, instilling us with fear and awe. However, this is not merely the feeling of being scared of Hashem. Rather, it is a type of fear and awe that ultimately translates into love, a *yirat haromemut* that is based on recognising Hashem's grandeur.

Although a human king is dependent on a nation and subjects, Hashem is intrinsically a King and is not dependent on anything. He ruled before anything was created. This means that He ruled over the nothingness that pre-dated creation.

On Rosh Hashanah, we proclaim Hashem as our King. *Adon Olam* is a microcosm of Rosh Hashanah, which we have available every single day. Reciting *Modeh Ani* in the morning also achieves that purpose. When we wake up in the morning and say *Modeh Ani,* we are, so to speak, anointing the King as soon as we wake up.

The Gemara in Berachot 5a says that a *Talmid Chacham* is exempt from the Bedtime Shema, but has to say at least one verse of *rachamim* (Divine mercy). As an example, it mentions the verse *b'yadecha afkid ruchi* (Tehillim 31:6). The conclusion of *Adon Olam* is based on this verse.

Many early commentators say that through saying *Adon Olam*, our prayers will be accepted. When saying *Adon Olam* before going to sleep, we are introducing extra merit into the prayers we will recite the next morning. Furthermore, we are connecting to the next morning after entrusting our souls to Hashem (*b'yado afkid ruchi*), as it then states *v'aira* – "and I will wake up".

CHAPTER 20: VIDDUY

Some people recite *vidduy* (confession of sins) at the end of the Bedtime Shema.

As on Yom Kippur, we must say *vidduy* standing and with a bowed head. When going through the sins in the alphabetical order, we should gently strike the left side of the chest with the right fist.

The *Zohar* explains that the Aleph to Tav order symbolizes the spiritual defilement that man has created in the universe. Chazal teach us that the universe was created with the Hebrew alphabet and that through repentance, man is aiming to rectify what he desecrated and defiled through his sins.

It is not enough to simply regret our past misdeeds, or even to make a sincere commitment to improve our ways. We must verbally specify which sins we committed and express truthful regret for our transgressions. The Aleph to Tav order means that various types of sins and transgressions are included.

In Pirkei Avot (2:15), Rabbi Eliezer says that a person should repent one day before his death. The Gemara (Shabbat 153a) relates that his disciples asked him, "How can a person know which day he will die?" He answered that since nobody knows the day of his death, a person should repent every day, as it is always possible that he will die the following day.

As we have seen, sleep is considered to be a sixtieth of death. Therefore, the end of the day, before going to sleep, is an opportune moment to say *vidduy* and repent for one's sins.

In Chapter 25, we will discuss halachic guidelines, including the days when *vidduy* is not said.

In some *siddurim,* including those which follow the *nusach* of the *Arizal*, extra prayers appear after *vidduy*.

CHAPTER 21: DAVID & BATSHEVA (PSALM 51)

Only some *siddurim* include this psalm, which is recited after *vidduy*.

(Parts of this chapter are taken from The Poetry of Prayer, Ch. 16, by Rabbi Avi Baumol, Gefen Publishing House).

The Book of Samuel II (Ch. 11 & 12) describes the union between King David and Batsheva. These chapters raise a number of questions that are complex from a philosophical and halachic point of view, and therefore beyond the scope of this chapter.

In Psalm 51, David describes the *teshuva* process he went through, which is why this psalm follows the *vidduy*. Most versions of the Bedtime Shema omit this psalm.

David, having been confronted and rebuked by the prophet Nathan, felt that he must confess his sin and beg for forgiveness. He did not look for justifications or excuses or try to cover up the incident. He repented publicly and openly by writing this psalm, describing his despair and his journey back to Hashem. As an aside, this represents a defining quality of leadership, rarely displayed by any leader before or after him.

The first step of *teshuvah* is recognising the sin, as it says in the psalm, "against You alone I have sinned".

The next step is to recognise one's weaknesses and their causes, and deciding in one's heart never to sin in this way again. Fundamentally, David writes that we are born with the capacity to sin. That same drive gives us the ability to overcome our weakness and inconsistency and rise to greatness and sublime spirituality. The sheer knowledge that we can obtain a clean slate with Hashem and a new beginning, gives us hope to continue the battle within ourselves.

The Gemara in Yoma 86b teaches that the power of *teshuvah* can erase sin. If one repents out of fear, his intentional sins change into unintentional sins. If he repents out of love, his sins turn into merits.

In the last section of this psalm, David asks, *Hashem s'fatai tiftach ufi yagid tehilatecha* - "Hashem! Open my lips and let my mouth declare Your praise". King David wanted to find a way to allow himself to open his mouth to speak to his Creator and move towards Him.

Hashem s'fatai tiftach ufi yagid tehilatecha is the way we start *Shemonei Esrei*. Surrender is essential in order to stand before Hashem. This includes fear, humility, subservience and even shame. Hashem is not interested in a constantly proud, self-righteous and overconfident individual standing before Him in prayer. Chazal remind us to surrender, to be humble, and to remember that a broken heart and crushed spirit have easier access to the Heavenly gates than an individual standing tall, praying and expecting an immediate answer.

In the Sephardi *nusach,* Psalm 25 is said after *vidduy* in Shacharit and Mincha. This is part of the *Tachanun* prayer. Ashkenazim recite Psalm 6 instead. Since *Tachanun* is not said at night, there is no reason to recite the psalm that is said as part of *Tachanun.*

Similarly, on Yom Kippur, when *Vidduy* is said but not *Tachanun*, these psalms are not said after *vidduy*. Psalm 51 is recited instead.

CHAPTER 22: ANA BECHO'ACH

Some people recite *Ana Becho'ach* towards the end of the Bedtime Shema.

(Parts of this chapter come from the introduction of an article by Rabbi Dov Ber Pinson (Iyyun - Centre for Jewish Spirituality, www.iyyun.com).)

In this prayer, attributed to the Tanna Rabbi Nechunya Ben Hakkana, we ask Hashem to protect the Jewish people and accept their prayers.

Ana Becho'ach as a whole represents a movement from one state to another. As explained in the Breslov *siddur* "Eit Ratzon", the purpose of the prayer is to elevate our actions in this world, known as *asiyah* (action), to a higher realm known as *yetzirah* (creation). It is comprised of seven verses, corresponding to the seven days of the week. The prayer is intended to elevate the days to a level beyond time and space. Each verse contains six words, corresponding to the six wings of the angels mentioned in Isaiah (6:2). It states there that the angel uses two wings to cover its face, two wings to cover its feet, and two wings to fly. R' Nachman of Breslov derives from here the correct way for a person to grow in serving Hashem. He should serve Hashem on the level he is on, and not jump prematurely to higher levels. He should also not consider serving Hashem on lower level than he is on, as such service is not sufficient for him. By keeping to these guidelines, the person will gradually be able to fly to higher spiritual levels. The two wings that cover the face symbolise how a person should not suddenly jump to higher levels. The two wings that cover the feet symbolise how a person should not sink to lower levels. The two wings that fly symbolise that as long as a person does not jump too fast to higher levels and does not give up hope, he will fly and soar towards spiritual heights.

The seven verses also correspond to the seven emotional *sefirot* through which the Divine energy sustains the universe. This energy itself was created in a seven-day cycle.

Ana Becho'ach represents the seven *sefirot* and for this reason is recited in prayers where there is a symbolic ascent of Divine energy from a lower plane to a higher one, or whenever there is any movement from one reality into the next.

This prayer contains 42 words, of which the first letters form the 42-letter Name of Hashem, according to the Arizal. The Gemara in Kiddushin 71a says that Hashem's 42-letter Name may only be taught to someone who is on a particularly high spiritual level. Rashi says that we no longer have a tradition about the identity of this Name. It seems that the Arizal revealed the identity of this Name, which had been hidden for centuries.

The connection to the Bedtime Shema is that in this prayer, we ask Hashem to protect us. This is something we particularly need when going to sleep at night.

The prayer also hints to Hashem's 42-letter Name, which provides protection.

Some have the custom to say only the verse that corresponds to the current day of the week. Others recite the entire prayer and then repeat the verse of the day three times.

At the end of the prayer, *Baruch Shem* is said. This sentence is recited whenever the unity of Hashem is expressed, such as after the first verse of Shema. In the *Bet Hamikdash*, it was said after the mention of Hashem's Name. In this case, we have mentioned Hashem's 42-letter Name through the acrostic. We see from this prayer that Hashem's 42-letter Name starts with aleph and ends with tav.

CHAPTER 23: FINAL VERSES

Some versions of the Bedtime Shema conclude with a number of verses. The verses described below are not an exhaustive list as there are varying customs. The common theme of all these verses is that they enable us to go to sleep with words of Torah on our minds and to stay connected to Hashem as we drift to sleep.

Gad gedud yegudenu vehu yagud akev.

A troop will troop forth from Gad and it will retreat in its tracks (Bereshit 49:19).

This verse comes from the blessing Yaakov gave to Gad before he died. Targum Onkelos and Rashi explain it to refer to the troops from the tribe of Gad who would march in front of the Israelite army in the conquest of the Land of Israel during the time of Yehoshua bin Nun. At the end of the conquest, they would return to their land on the east bank of the Jordan River without having lost a single soldier. Ibn Ezra explains the verse to mean, "Troops will attack Gad, but he will defeat them in the end". According to both explanations, the verse refers to Hashem's protection, so it is fitting to recite it before going to sleep.

Im tishkav lo tifchad veshchavta ve'areva shenatecha.

When you lie down, you will not fear. You will lie down and your sleep will be pleasant (Mishlei 3:24).

Rabbeinu Yonah explains this verse to be referring to a person who observes the Torah. Hashem causes the Torah to protect him not only when he is awake but even when he is asleep.

Furthermore, he is not only protected from physical harm but also from disturbing dreams.

Betov alin ve'akitz berachamim.

May I sleep well and awaken with Your mercy.

This phrase comes from P'ri Etz Chaim by R' Chaim Vital. Rabbi Rashi Simon (Kesher, London) believes that it is based on pesukim from the final chapter of Daniel, which discusses the End of Days. It says in verse 8, "Velo avin" (and I do not understand). The term alin (I will lie down) might be a play on the word avin. The term ve'akitz (and I will awake) might be a play on the word ketz (end) in verse 13, which refers to the time when the dead will arise at the End of Days.

Liyshuatecha kiviti Hashem

I hope in Your salvation Hashem (Bereishit 49:18).

See Chapter 15 for explanations.

Lefurkanach sabarit Hashem.

I hope in Your salvation Hashem.

This is Onkelos' Targum (Aramaic translation) for the previous verse.

Ata seter li mitzar titsereni ronei falet tesoveveni selah.

You are my shelter, You protect me from distress, with songs of deliverance You surround me, Selah! (Tehillim 32:7).

The verse is a prayer by King David to be constantly protected from enemies and troubles. Metzudat David explains that David promised that whenever he would be saved from trouble, he would always sing to Hashem for being saved. The word "Selah" means forever.

The same verse is then repeated word for word but in reversed order. This is similar to the verse *liyshuatecha kiviti Hashem,* which is repeated in three different orders. The change of order has Kabbalistic connotations.

Todieni orach chaim sova semachot et panecha neimot biminecha netzach.

You will make known to me the path of life, the fullness of joys in Your presence, the delights that are in Your right hand for eternity (Tehillim 16:11)

Rashi explains that this verse refers to the World to Come, where the joy will be eternal. Metzudat David explains that we pray to Hashem to teach us the right way to behave, which will lead to eternal life and joy in the World to Come.

Ata takum terachem Tzion ki eit lechenenah ki va moed.

You will arise and have mercy on Zion, for it is time to be gracious to her, for the appointed time has come (Tehillim 102:14)

Radak explains that in this verse, we express our trust that Hashem will rebuild Jerusalem and the Temple, even though it is a very long time since it was destroyed. Although Hashem brought about the destruction, He will have mercy and bring about the Redemption.

Beyadecha afkid ruchi padita oti Hashem el emet.

In Your hand I entrust my spirit, You redeem me, Hashem, G-d of truth (Tehillim 31:6).

Radak explains that King David was expressing his trust that Hashem would always save him from his enemies. He called Hashem "G-d of truth" in order to show his faith in Hashem's word that he would be king of the Jewish people despite all those who tried to prevent this.

Ben Ish Chai writes (Section 1, *Parshat Pekudei*) that there is great Kabbalistic significance in the words of this verse, as well as the words of the verse *Ata seter li*. They hint to mystical Divine names.

Torah tziva lanu Moshe morasha kehilat Yaakov.

The Torah that Moshe commanded us is an inheritance of the congregation of Jacob (Devarim 33:4).

This verse comes from the blessing that Moshe gave the Jewish people before his death. He described the revelation that took place when the Torah was given. Rashi explains that in this verse, he was reminding the Jewish people of their commitment to grasp on to the Torah and never forsake it. Chazal teach us that this is the first verse that a father should teach his son once he learns to speak (Sifri, quoted in Rashi to Devarim 11:19).

Some repeat this at least seven times or until they fall asleep.

David melech yisrael chai ve kayam.

David, King of Israel, lives and endures.

This verse comes from the Gemara in Rosh Hashanah 25a and is said in the Kiddush Levanah prayer. It is based on the blessing that Batsheva gave to King David before his death, when he confirmed that her son Shlomo would be the next king. It states (I Kings 1:31), "Batsheva prostrated herself with her face to the ground and bowed down to the king, and she said, May my master King David live forever!" Radak explain this to refer to his life in the World to Come. It cannot refer to this world, as he was about to die.

In the Gemara, Rabbi Yehudah Hanasi asked Rabbi Chiya to use this verse as a code that he had sanctified the New Moon. Rashi explains that King David is compared to the moon. This is probably because in the same way as the moon waxes and wanes and waxes again, the Davidic Kingdom was powerful in its time, lost its power when the first Temple was destroyed, and will regain its power when Mashiach comes, speedily in our days.

It is customary to repeat this verse twelve times.

Or zarua latsadik ulyishrei lev simcha.

Light is sown for the righteous and joy for the upright of heart (Tehillim 97:11)

Mezudat David explains that this verse refers to the reward in the World to Come. In the same way as a person plants seeds and they produce a far greater quantity of produce than the volume of the seeds themselves, Hashem provides a righteous person far more reward for his good deeds than he would have received if he would have been rewarded immediately.

CHAPTER 24: PSALMS 1-4

Some men recite Psalms 1-4 before going to sleep. They are said as a *segulah* to be protected from a nocturnal emission, which causes a person to become ritually impure with the *tumah* of *keri*. The source of reciting them is the Shelah. There are 306 words in these psalms. Together with the number four, which is the number of psalms said, the total number is 310, which is the *gematria* of the word *keri*. Therefore, the recital of the psalms protects a person from *keri*. Even people who did not say these psalms every night say them at the end of davening on Yom Kippur night, as it is particularly important to remain ritually pure on the holy day of Yom Kippur.

CHAPTER 25: HALACHIC CONSIDERATIONS

(All references to the *Shulchan Aruch* and *Rema* are from *Orach Chaim*).

The following are taken from the *Kitzur Shulchan Aruch* (Chapter 71) unless otherwise stated, and are for guidance only. A competent halachic authority should be consulted for a final decision.

It is sufficient for a healthy person to sleep six hours per night. However, Rambam writes (*Hilchot De'ot* 4:4) that it is sufficient for a person to sleep eight hours per night. (See more about this in the introduction). The *Mishnah Berurah* (238:2) writes that there is no set measure for sleep for all people. The hours of sleep are set according to each person's health and needs. Nevertheless, one should not indulge in too much sleep. According to the Steipler, a person should sleep seven hours per night.

A person should be careful not to sleep in a room alone and not to sleep in a place that is too hot or too cold.

It is proper for every G-d fearing man, before going to sleep, to examine the deeds he performed that day. If he finds that he committed a transgression, he should regret it, confess it and wholeheartedly resolve not to do it again.

A person should also resolve to forgive any person who sinned against him, so that no person should be punished because of him.

If a person did not recite the three paragraphs of *Keriat Shema* after nightfall, he should say all three paragraphs during the Bedtime Shema. If he already recited them at night, he only needs to recite the first paragraph. Nevertheless, it is meritorious to recite all three paragraphs again.

If a person cannot sleep, he should recite *Keriat Shema* again, followed by psalms and verses of mercy, until he falls asleep.

In most *siddurim*, *Hamapil* is printed before *Keriat Shema*. However, it is preferable to say it at the end so that it immediately precedes sleep. On the other hand, the *Mishnah Berurah* lists three options but does not rule which one to follow. See Chapter 2 for further details.

A person should not sleep in his day clothes nor place his clothes under his head, because such actions cause a person to forget his learning.

It is advisable to begin sleeping on the left side and finish on the right side. This is beneficial for one's health because the liver is located onto the right side and the stomach on the left. When leaning on the left, the liver rests on the stomach and warms it, thereby facilitating digestion. After the food has been digested, it is advisable to turn on the right side so that the stomach rests and causes waste to pass through. One should not turn from side to side too often during the night.

It is forbidden for a man to lie flat on his back or on his front.

The *Ben Ish Chai* (Section 1, Pekudei 14) says that one who intends to remain awake the entire night (e.g. Shavuot or Hoshana Rabba), should recite the Bedtime Shema in full close to midnight. *Hamapil* should be omitted, as it is only said when a person goes to sleep.

The *Kaf Hachaim* (239:3) states that it is the custom of women and girls to recite the Bedtime Shema as it acts as a protection and *tikkun* to the soul.

After reciting the Bedtime Shema, one should not eat or drink. One who found it necessary to eat should repeat at least the first paragraph of *Keriat Shema*.

According to the *Shulchan Aruch* (3:6, 240:17), the bed that a man sleeps in with his wife should face from north to south, not from east to west. *Mishnah Berurah* (3:11) writes that the head of the bed should be in the north and the foot of the bed in the south. It is preferable to do this even when sleeping by oneself. According to *Menachem Azariah,* the *Zohar* holds the opposite of the *Shulchan Aruch* (according to the *Zohar*, the bed should face from east to west). The Vilna Gaon disputes this, and holds that the *Zohar* agrees with the *Shulchan Aruch*. *Kaf Hachaim* (3:16) holds that the *Zohar* disagrees with the *Shulchan Aruch* and that one should ideally follow the *Zohar* in this matter. Therefore, according to the *Kaf Hachaim,* although one may place one's bed in any direction, as there is a strong basis for both opinions, it is preferable to follow the *Zohar* and put the head of the bed in the east and the foot of the bed in the west.

There is a custom not to sleep with one's feet directly facing a door as this position gives the impression that one is about to be taken out of the room (i.e. a dead body).

The *Mishnah Berurah* (2:11) says in the name of the Shelah that it is correct to sleep with a *kippah* on one's head. *Rema* (21:3) mentions an opinion that one should not wear a *tallit katan* when going to sleep, as this might be considered disrespectful to the mitzvah. However, *Rema* concludes that this in permitted. According to the Arizal, a person should sleep with a *tallit katan* (*Mishnah Berurah*). This is based on Kabbalistic teachings. Many people follow this custom.

During the day, a person should refrain from sleeping more than *Shitin Nishmin* ("sixty breaths") (*Shulchan Aruch* and *Rema* 4:16). *Bei'ur Halacha* writes that some say that this is slightly more than three minutes, others say half an hour, while others say three hours. In any case, a person should be careful not to sleep for a significant amount of time during the day unless this will help him to serve Hashem more effectively.

However, on Shabbat a person is allowed to sleep longer during the day, but should not sleep too much, as that will take time away from learning Torah.

Hamapil is not recited before sleeping during the day (*Mishnah Berurah* 29:8).

One should not keep food under a bed, due a concern of *ruach ra'ah* (harmful spirits).

For those who say *Vidduy*, it should be said while standing. One should repent for his sins and accept upon himself not to repeat the transgression. *Vidduy* should not be recited on Shabbat or Yom Tov. The Kaf Hachaim (239:2) cites the custom of not saying *Vidduy* on the days when *Tachanun* is not recited and also at the end of those days until *Chatzot* (midnight).

Piskei Teshuvot (239:3) writes that after saying the Bedtime Shema, a person is allowed to say *Birkat Halevanah*. It does not make any difference why he did not say it earlier. For example, the moon may have been obscured by clouds or he might have forgotten to say it. He also writes, based on various sources, that if a person went to the bathroom after the Bedtime Shema, he should recite *Asher Yatzar*. Similarly, if a person forgot to daven Maariv or count *Sefirat Ha'Omer*, he should do so even after he said the Bedtime Shema.

According to the *Rema* (481:2) and *Mishnah Berurah* (481:4), on the night of the Pesach Seder, only *Hamapil* and the first paragraph of Shema should be recited, as the first night of Pesach is a night of protection from danger (see Shemot 12:42). Outside *Eretz Yisrael,* this also applies on the second night on Pesach according to most opinions.

CHAPTER 26: CONCLUSION

King Solomon writes in Mishlei (Proverbs) 3:6, *b'chol derachecha da'ehu*, "In all your ways, know Him (Hashem)". *Metzudat David* explains that whatever a person does, he should have in mind that he is doing it in order to serve Hashem better. The verse concludes that if a person does this, "He (Hashem) will straighten your path". Therefore, he will be successful in everything he does.

Having discovered numerous insights of the Bedtime Shema, it is clear that falling asleep can be much more than a physical state. A seemingly mundane activity can be elevated to a highly spiritual experience.

Reciting the Bedtime Shema should only take 10 to 15 minutes, but this is very valuable time as it is spent in an important spiritual pursuit.

It serves as a protection against harmful spiritual forces (*mazikim*) and ensures that we fall asleep with words of Torah on our minds. Finally, it connects the end of the day to the next day and recharges a person physically and spiritually.

For any comments, observations or further contributions, please e-mail hamapil.shema@gmail.com

BIBLIOGRAPHY

Alshich: Commentary on Tanach written by Rabbi Moshe Alshich, a Rabbinic leader in Tzefat during the 16th century.

Arizal: Rabbi Isaac Luria Ashkenazi, 1534-1572. Lived in Tzefat and is considered the father of contemporary Kabbalah.

Baal Haturim: A brief commentary on the Torah, based mainly on gematria and remazim (hints), by Rav Yaakov ben Rabbenu Asher (c. 1275-c. 1340, Germany, Spain). His most famous work was his Halachic compendium, Arba Turim, better known as the Tur.

Beis Halevi: Rabbi Yosef Dov Soloveitchik (1820-1892, Russia). He was a descendent of Rabbi Chaim Volozhin and was one of the Roshei Yeshiva in Volozhin Yeshiva. He was subsequently the Rabbi of Slutzk and Brisk. He wrote works on Halacha and Chumash.

Ben Ish Chai: A collection of the laws of everyday life interspersed with mystical insights and customs, arranged according the weekly Torah portion, written by Rabbi Yosef Chaim (1835-1909, Baghdad, Iraq).

Breslov Siddur "Eit Ratzon": Siddur with commentary based on Breslov Chassidic sources, published by the Breslov Chassidic community of Jerusalem.

Chazal: Acronym for *chachameinu zichronam livracha* - our Sages of blessed memory. This refers to the teaching of the Sages mentioned in the Talmud and Midrash.

Ibn Ezra: Rabbi Abraham ben Meir (1089-1167, Spain), one of the most important biblical commentators (Hebrew grammar in particular) and philosophers of the Middle Ages.

Kaf Hachaim: A work of Halacha written by Rabbi Yaakov Chaim Sofer (1870-1939, Baghdad, Jerusalem).

Kitzur Shulchan Aruch: A work of Halacha by Rabbi Shlomo Ganzfried (1804-1886, Hungary)

Kli Yakar: Commentary on the Chumash by Rabbi Shlomo Ephraim Lunschitz (c.1550-1619, Lemberg and Prague).

Maharsha. Commentary on the Talmud by Rabbi Shlomo Eidels (1555-1632, Poland).

Mechilta, Sifri. A compilation from the Tannaic disciples of Rabbi Akiva, who lived in Eretz Yisrael during the 2nd century CE, mainly Halachic in nature, written as a commentary on the Chumash. Mechilta is the commentary on Shemot, Sifra is the commentary on Vayikra, and Sifri is the commentary on Bamidbar and Devarim.

Metzudat David: Rabbi David Altschuler, an 18th century biblical commentator, who lived in Poland. He wrote a commentary on Nevi'im and Ketuvim.

Midrash: Rabbinic literature that offers commentary or interpretation of biblical texts by the Talmudic sages (mainly 1st-6th centuries CE). The most well-known Midrashim include Midrash Rabba and Midrash Tanchuma.

Mishna Berura: A Halachic commentary written by the Chofetz Chaim (Rabbi Yisrael Meir Kagan, 1838-1933, Poland), on Orach Chaim (the first section of the Shulchan Aruch) which deals with laws of prayer, synagogue, Shabbat and holidays. This work includes the commentaries Be'iur Halacha and Shaar Hatziyun.

Netziv: Rabbi Naftali Tzvi Yehuda Berlin (1817-1893), Rosh Yeshivah of Volozhin, Lithuania. He wrote a commentary on Chumash called Haamek Davar, a commentary on the Talmud called Meromei Sadeh and a commentary on the She'eltot (a Gaonic work) called Haamek Shaalah.

Ohr Hachaim: A commentary on the Torah by Rabbi Chaim ben Moshe Ibn Attar (1696-1743, Italy, Morocco and Jerusalem).

Pirkei D'Rabbi Eliezer: An Aggadic-Midrashic work on the Torah containing exegesis and retellings of biblical stories based on the teachings of the Tanna Rabbi Eliezer (1st-2nd century CE) and his disciples.

Piskei Teshuvot: A contemporary Halachic work by Rabbi Simcha Ben-Tzion Isaac Rabinowitz (Israel), arranged according to the order of Shulchan Aruch Orach Chaim and Mishnah Berurah.

P'ri Etz Chaim: A Kabbalistic work by R' Chaim Vital (1543-1620, Israel, Syria), a disciple of the Arizal.

Rabbi Avraham Palagi: Lived in Izmir, Turkey (1809-1898), where he was the Chief Rabbi (Chacham Bashi). He was the son of Rabbi Chaim Palagi. He wrote numerous books in Hebrew and Ladino.

Rabbenu Bachya: Rabbi Bachya ben Asher Ibn Halawa (1255-1340, Spain), who wrote a classic commentary on the Torah. Not to be confused with Rabbenu Bachya ben Yosef ibn Paquda, rabbi and philosopher (1050-1120, Spain).

Rabbi Moshe Shapiro: Leading Rabbinic thinker and lecturer in Eretz Yisrael (1935-2017).

Rabbeinu Yonah: Rabbi Yonah ben Avraham Gerondi (c. 1180-1263, Spain). Torah leader of his generation, wrote commentaries on Talmud, Rif, the Book of Mishlei (Proverbs). Author of classic Mussar work "Shaarei Teshuvah".

Rabbi Abraham Twerski: contemporary American Rabbi and psychiatrist. Wrote several books on Jewish topics and on self-help.

Rabbi Nechunya Ben Hakkana: Lived during 1st/2nd century CE and is considered one of the greatest masters of Kabbalah. He was one of the Tannaim of the Mishnah.

Radak: Rabbi David Kimche (1160-1235, Provence, France) was a biblical commentator, philosopher and grammarian.

Rambam: Rabbi Moshe ben Maimon (1135-1204, Spain-Egypt), a.k.a. Maimonides, one of the most prolific and influential Torah scholars of the Middle Ages. He was also a preeminent astronomer and physician. He wrote a commentary on the Mishnah, a Halachic compendium called Mishnah Torah or Yad Hachazakah and the Guide to the Perplexed (Moreh Nevuchim). Maimonides formulated his "13 principles of faith", a summary of what he viewed as the required beliefs of Judaism. These can be found in most siddurim.

Ramban: Rabbi Moshe ben Nachman (1194-1270, Spain-Eretz Yisrael), a.k.a Nachmanides. A foremost Torah leader and kabbalist. He wrote many Torah works, including a commentary on the Chumash.

Ramchal: Rabbi Moshe Chaim ben Luzzato (1707-1746, Italy), a prominent scholar, kabbalist, and philosopher. His main works are Messilat Yesharim, Derech Hashem and Da'at Tevunot.

Rashi: Rabbi Shlomo Yitzchaki (1040-1105, France). Author of a comprehensive commentary on the Talmud and on the Tanach. His works remain a fundamental of contemporary Jewish study.

R' Nachman of Breslov: Founder and leader of Breslov Chassidim (1772-1810, Poland-Ukraine), authored various works on Torah and Chassidic thought.

Rema: Rabbi Moshe Isserles (1530-1572, Poland) was a renowned Talmudic and legal scholar. He was the primary halakhic authority for European Jewry of his day. He is best known for his notes to the Shulchan Aruch, discussing cases where Sephardi and Ashkenazi customs differ.

Seforno: Rabbi Ovadia ben Yaakov Sforno (1470-1550, Italy) was a biblical commentator, philosopher and physician.

Shelah Hakadosh: An encyclopaedic compilation of ritual, ethics, and mysticism written by Rabbi Yeshayahu ben Avraham Horowitz (1560-1630, Poland, Frankfort, Prague, Jerusalem, Tiberias).

Shlomo Ibn Gabirol: 11th-century Spanish poet and philosopher. He published over a hundred poems, as well as works of biblical exegesis, philosophy and ethics.

Shulchan Aruch: Code of Jewish Law, is the most widely consulted legal code in Judaism. It was authored by Rav Yosef Karo of Spain, Turkey and Tzefat (1488-1575). Together with its commentaries, it is the most widely accepted compilation of Jewish law ever written. The rulings generally follow Sephardic law and customs.

Steipler: Rabbi Yaakov Yisrael Kanievski (1899-1985, Hornisteipel, Novardok, B'nei B'rak). Torah leader and Talmudic commentator.

Targum: Aramaic translation and interpretation of the scriptures. The two most important ones are Targum Onkelos on the Torah by the proselyte Onkelos, composed around the end of the first century CE, and Targum Yonatan on the Nevi'im (Prophets), composed by the Tanna Rabbi Yonatan ben Uzziel in 1st century CE. There is also a Targum known as Targum Yonatan on the Torah. Evidence suggests that it was written after 4th century CE.

Toldos Aharon: A compilation of sources connected to pessukim of Tanach. It is printed in many Chumashim. It was compiled by R' Aharon of Pizaro in Italy during the 16th century

Tosafot: A commentary on the Talmud by the leading Torah scholars of France in 12th and 13th centuries. They take the form of critical and explanatory notes, printed, in almost all Talmud editions, on the outer margin and opposite Rashi's notes.

Vilna Gaon: Rabbi Eliyahu ben Shlomo Zalman, a.k.a. the Gra (1720-1797, Poland-Russia) was a Talmudist, halachist, kabbalist, and the foremost leader of non-Chassidic Eastern European Jewry of the past few centuries. He was a prolific author, writing on all aspects of Judaism.

Zohar: The foundational work in the literature of Jewish mystical thought known as Kabbalah. It includes a commentary on the mystical aspects of the Torah and scriptural interpretations as well as material on mysticism, mythical cosmogony, and mystical psychology. It also includes non-mystical explanations.

Zohar Chadash. This is part of the Zohar that was not included in the original printed edition.

Printed in Great Britain
by Amazon